Death and the Adolescent

Judy Oaks, Ed.D., Director
Center for Personal Recovery
Berea, Kentucky

GLENCOE

McGraw-Hill

New York, New York   Columbus, Ohio   Mission Hills, California   Peoria, Illinois

Consultants

Kathryn Descarpentrie
Curriculum Director
Wheaton Warrenville Community Unit School District 200
Wheaton, Illinois

Joanna Hart, Ph.D.
Psychologist, Consultant
Hospice at Riverside
Columbus, Ohio

Send all inquiries to:
Glencoe/McGraw-Hill
15319 Chatsworth Street
P.O. Box 9609
Mission Hills, CA 91346-9609

ISBN 0-02-651512-1   Death and the Adolescent

Printed in the United States of America.

1 2 3 4 5 6 7 8 9 MAL   01 00 99 98 97 96 95

C O N T E N T S

CHAPTER 1: INTRODUCTION AND BACKGROUND 1

How We Grieve 1   What Affects How We Mourn? 4

How Long Should We Mourn? 3   Teens and Death 6

CHAPTER 2: HOW SCHOOLS CAN HELP 8

Schools Need To Help 8   The Case of Franklin High 11

What Schools Can Do 8

CHAPTER 3: WHAT TEACHERS CAN DO 13

Help Bereaved Students 13   Recognize When Professional
Help Is Needed 15

**CHAPTER 4: TEACHING STRATEGIES AND
ACTIVITIES FOR GRIEF RECOVERY** 16

Objectives: Expressing Feelings 16

Activities

Dealing With Loss 16   *Fill in the Blanks* 17

The Life Continuum 16   *Unfinished Business* 18

Listen/Communicate 17   *Expressing Feelings* 18

Facts and Feelings 17

Objectives: Helping Others 16

Activities

Helping Qualities 18   *Comfort Zone* 18

Dos and Don'ts 18   *Sympathy/Empathy* 18

APPENDIX

RESOURCES 19

Organizations 19   Books (fiction) 20

Books (nonfiction) 19

INTRODUCTION AND BACKGROUND

The purpose of this book is to provide information on how death affects people, particularly teens, and the best ways to help them through the stages of mourning. The book describes how schools can function in responding quickly and effectively to deaths of students or staff members. It helps teachers recognize when their students may need professional help in dealing with death-related emotional stress. Finally, it suggests teaching strategies that will encourage students to gain knowledge and skills to cope with death in a healthy way.

Why is a book like this necessary? A major reason is that our culture is death-denying—we fear death, we avoid talking about it, and few of us know how to deal with it. Children, especially, tend to be sheltered from death in attempts to protect them from emotional pain. This is unfortunate, because denying death prevents us from fully experiencing our loss, processing our grief, and healing our emotional pain. By ignoring death, psychological problems, including depression, suicide, drug use, poor self-esteem, and school failure may result.

The school bus had stopped on the highway in front of Roy's house. Roy ran from the bus to cross the road just as a car raced by from the opposite direction, ignoring the flashing red lights of the bus. The car struck Roy and dragged him several yards down the road. Roy died instantly of massive head and internal injuries. The horrifying scene was witnessed by most of the 40 high school students on the bus, many of them Roy's friends and neighbors.

Ana had been dating Juan for several weeks. Ana's parents didn't approve of the relationship and finally forbade Ana from seeing Juan again. The two teens ran away together, parked Juan's car in an abandoned barn, and then set the barn on fire. Ana and Juan died in the conflagration. Their high school is flooded with rumors about how and why the tragedy occurred. Their closest classmates are extremely distraught, and parents and teachers are worried about "copy-cat" suicides.

Jamahl Brown was one of the finest teachers and well-liked staff member at Harrison High School. He was a young man, in his early 30s, so everyone was shocked when they found out that Jamahl had been diagnosed with a brain tumor. His doctor gave him less than 6 months to live. He deteriorated rapidly and had to be hospitalized after 2 months. A few weeks later, the hospital notified the principal that Jamahl had died.

Deaths such as those just described could easily happen to students and staff in your school. How would you, as a teacher or administrator, respond to such tragic deaths? How would you help your students cope with their feelings of grief, fear, and loss? What could your school do? Does it have a plan, already in place, to quickly and effectively deal with events like these?

Most likely the answer to these questions is "no." Suicides, homicides, and accidental deaths are increasing at alarming rates in our teen population, yet many teachers and schools have little information and training to help students (and staff) deal with such tragic events.

How We Grieve

To help you understand and support your students when they're grieving a death, it's important to become familiar with the grieving process—how we come to accept the death, deal with the painful emotions it causes, and recover from our grief. Bereavement expert William Worden describes this process as "the four tasks of mourning":

- accepting the death;
- reviewing experiences with the deceased and experiencing the feelings associated with the loss;
- refilling all the roles and reassigning all the responsibilities of the deceased;
- reinvesting in living without the deceased.

Keep in mind that, while it's easier to discuss grieving by referring to these four stages, we actually experience our grief as a continuous process that may not proceed in neat stages. We may even experience two or more stages of mourning simultaneously. We also can experience the stages more than once.

Task One: Accepting the Reality

Before healing can begin, the reality of the death must be accepted. For this reason, all those who were closely acquainted with the deceased need to know the facts surrounding the death, although explicit details and graphic descriptions are not necessary and may be psychologically traumatizing.

When someone close to us dies, we may be numbed by the shock of the death, feeling little if anything at first. Accepting the fact of the death may take some time. For most people, attending the funeral and viewing the body help make the death real. For some people, however, the shock of death may be so great that they cannot accept it for weeks or even months after the funeral. Such denial is a self-protective device that's healthy for awhile but indicative that help is needed if denial is prolonged.

Some people respond to the death of someone close to them by repeatedly discussing or asking about details of the death and what led up to it. They try to see how the death might have been avoided. They seem to be searching for validation that the death actually occurred.

The behavior shown by Chen's friends and Victor's brother in the following two examples is typical of individuals who are struggling to accept the reality of a death.

Chen, a high school senior, lost control of his car after leaving basketball practice at school. He ran off the road, crashed into a tree, and died instantly of a broken neck. Students at school were told this much about Chen's death, but it didn't satisfy several of his closest friends. They went to the scene of the accident after school to try to see for themselves how it had happened and to search for clues as to why Chen lost control of his car.

Victor's accident occurred only 500 yards from his house. Witnesses said he was not speeding but had pulled off the road for some reason. The soft shoulder caused his wheels to lock and his truck to flip over. After a lengthy investigation, a piece of metal from a previous accident was determined to be the cause of the accident. Apparently, Victor hit the metal in the roadway and pulled off to examine his new truck for damage. Even with this information, Victor's 14-year-old brother still fantasized that someone ran Victor's truck off the road. It was too hard for him to accept that something so meaningless as a piece of scrap metal could lead to his brother's death.

Task Two: Reviewing Experiences and Experiencing Feelings

The second task of mourning involves reviewing one's life experiences with the deceased and experiencing the emotional pain of the loss. It's normal to feel a wide range of emotions in this stage of grieving.

We're most likely to feel sad over the loss, but it's not uncommon to feel anger—anger toward the doctors who failed to save the life, anger toward God who seemed so cruel to take the life, or anger toward the deceased for dying and causing us such pain. Some people may feel fear, because death reminds them of their own mortality and that of loved ones. The death of someone very close may even lead us to feel abandoned.

Some people may feel regret when a loved one dies—regret over things they may have said or done to the deceased or regret for the life experiences they no longer have the opportunity to share. In the case of terminal illness, some people may feel relief that the suffering has ended, but this may be accompanied by feelings of guilt because the feelings of relief seem selfish and wrong. Resentment is another common feeling experienced by bereaved individuals. They may resent others for failing to understand the pain of their loss, for seeming so carefree, and for still having their families intact (but not appreciating them). Note that when some people are feeling extreme grief, they may laugh instead of cry, even though there is no joy in their hearts.

Emotional pain is a necessary step in processing the loss of a loved one, provided we have the freedom to express our feelings and have them validated as normal. Unfortunately, many people attempt to repress their feelings, and this hampers the recovery process. One reason we repress our feelings is that, in our culture, expression of strong feelings often makes others feel uncomfortable. Males, especially, tend to bottle up their feelings inside, after years of conditioning "to be strong" and "act like a man." Teens in dysfunctional families are very likely to have been taught to repress their feelings and deny the more painful aspects of reality, including the feelings of loss associated with death. They are likely to have a particularly difficult time recovering from loss.

Task Three: Readjusting Roles and Responsibilities

The third task of mourning requires the bereaved to make the necessary adjustment to living without the deceased. All roles and responsibilities held by the deceased will need to be fulfilled by someone else. A sibling may have to take on more responsibilities at home. A new student using the deceased's locker or a new teacher in the classroom serves as a reminder of the deceased person's absence. These reminders may result in a variety of reactions. Some people may feel anger and frustration toward those attempting to fill the roles of the deceased. The bereaved may need affirmation that all human beings are unique, including the deceased, and that no one can be replaced by anyone else.

Task Four: Reinvesting in Life

The fourth task of mourning is to withdraw emotional energy from the deceased and to reinvest it in other people or activities. For weeks or even months after a death, it's normal to feel that you'll never get over the loss. In truth, we may never reach a point in time when all thoughts about the individual are totally free of emotional pain. However, the emotional pain should not cripple us to the point that we are afraid to risk loving again. When we put effort into loving another person or in some other way involve ourselves whole-heartedly in life again, we demonstrate that we have completed the fourth task of mourning.

How Long Should We Mourn?

We have a myth in our society that one should be recovered emotionally from a death at the end of one year. In reality, the average length of time for completion of mourning is about two and a half years, and the time varies greatly from person to person. Many people experience difficulty for several years following a major loss. Some people never complete the process of grieving and grieve for a lifetime. It's not true that "time heals all wounds." Only by working through the four stages of mourning can we heal the emotional wounds of the loss.

Ironically, the one-year anniversary of a death may be one of the most painful days for the bereaved. A return of depression, a drop in performance, and an increase in illness, irritability, and emotional sensitivity may occur around the anniversary of the death. Birthdays and holidays are likely to be especially difficult as well. This type of response is normal and should be validated as such.

Dysfunctional Mourning—When Grief Goes Wrong

If all goes well, the outcome of the mourning process is healing, recovery, and renewal of our investment in life. For a variety of reasons, however, sometimes grief goes wrong. This is referred to as dysfunctional mourning. Dysfunctional responses to death include chronic, inhibited, and delayed grief. Chronic grief is abnormally long and intense. Inhibited grief characterizes the individual who represses the death and emotional pain. Delayed grief is grief that does not occur until weeks or even years after the death occurred.

In dysfunctional mourning, the bereaved individual may experience any or all of the following:

- intense emotions;
- preoccupation with the deceased;
- denial of the loss by organizing life as though the deceased person will come back;
- emergence of unresolved past losses;
- dissatisfaction and ill temper with friends, family, and self;
- manifestation of disease symptoms that led to death of the deceased;
- severe depression (demonstrated by insomnia, nightmares, loss of interest in former

activities, poor personal health care, poor memory, or muddled thinking);

- intense separation anxiety;
- self-destructive behavior;
- outbursts of anger and bitterness;
- intense ambivalence;
- idealization of the deceased;
- intense anniversary reactions.

What Affects How We Mourn?

How successfully we heal our emotional pain after a death depends on many variables. Emotional support is probably the most important way to prevent dysfunctional mourning. With the help of loving, nurturing others, we can accept the reality of the loss, talk out our emotional pain, and recover from our grief.

The Family

Although the family has the potential to be the bereaved's greatest source of emotional support, the family may in fact be a source of additional stress, leading to dysfunctional grieving. The presence of several grieving people in one household can be very stressful in itself. Family members may be experiencing different feelings, as they grieve the loss at their own pace. Communication is often strained. It's not surprising that marital discord and family conflicts occur in a high percentage of families after a death.

As family members are preoccupied with their own grief, they're likely to have less support to give each other than they usually give. This is especially likely if one parent dies, leaving the surviving parent with added parenting responsibilities in addition to the grief. If a grandparent has played a parental role in the family, his or her death may be equally devastating. Consider the case of Chris.

*C*hris and her mom had lived with her grandmother since she was a baby. While her mom worked fulltime, Chris' grandma took care of her just like a mother—and she felt as close to her grandma as to her mom. Few people at school knew how close Chris was to her. When her grandma died of a sudden heart attack last year, everyone was surprised that she showed such strong emotions over the death. They didn't realize that Chris needed extra support during her grief.

Her mom was too greatly affected by the death to give Chris the additional support she needed. Chris became really depressed because no one seemed to understand or care how much it hurt her to lose her grandma.

The death of a child in the family is very distressing because the loss seems unfair and unnatural. The potential contribution to society the young person might have made is lost forever. If the death was that of an infant, the significance of the death may be overlooked by the community, thus inhibiting the expression and acknowledgment of the pain the family is suffering. When an older sibling dies, younger children may be greatly affected, as they mourn the loss of their protector, confidant, role model, and idol. The death of anyone at a young age will make younger people painfully aware of their own vulnerability to death.

Because losing a child is so difficult, a number of unhealthy responses are likely in families with deceased children. Idealization of a deceased child is one. It can negatively impact the sense of importance and self-esteem of surviving children. Another unhealthy response is "replacement" of the deceased by transference of expectations to surviving children, which can place a heavy psychological burden on the survivors. Some bereaved parents overindulge their surviving children in an effort to ease their own guilt and soothe the children's emotional pain.

How the family disposes of the possessions of the deceased child can reflect unhealthy responses. Keeping all the possessions of the deceased in place or creating a "shrine" is one extreme. The opposite extreme is the immediate disposition of all possessions without family discussion. A healthier response is a gradual giving up of possessions until only those remain that have significant meaning to family members. Siblings can maintain a sense of connection with the deceased by being allowed to keep prized possessions that are associated with positive memories of the deceased.

When more than one family member dies simultaneously, as sometimes happens in accidents, or when one family member dies within a short time of another's death, survivors may experience bereavement overload. It may take many years to recover emotionally from multiple deaths.

For those families that are dysfunctional prior to a death, it's possible that the death may lead to intervention and healing. It's more likely, however, that the family will experience dysfunctional mourning. Delayed and inhibited grief responses occur frequently in dysfunctional families, particularly those in which codependent behavior prevails. Children in such families may lack nurturing, emotional support, and adult models of appropriate coping skills. Such families tend to hide their feelings and fail to communicate in a meaningful way. Some children may block the memory of painful events. The new trauma of a recent death may result in flashbacks to the earlier painful events or in intense feelings of emotional pain that have no conscious cause. Cheryl's case shows how grieving can be delayed if intense emotions are repressed.

When Cheryl was seven, her mother was diagnosed with cancer. She died when Cheryl was eight. Cheryl was never allowed to visit her mother in the hospital before she died. During the funeral, Cheryl was sent to a friend's house to play. Her father forbade Cheryl from visiting the cemetery and has always refused to talk with Cheryl about her mother's death. Eight years later, Cheryl still has tremendous conflict over the fact that she played with other children during her mother's funeral. Cheryl is now receiving professional counselling.

For the grief recovery process to be completed successfully, a person must work through feelings regarding past losses as well as the recent death. Professional counseling, as in Cheryl's case, may be needed to guide the process of recovery so that the individual will experience healing of his or her emotional pain.

The Nature of the Death

The nature of the death, whether due to a suicide, homicide, accident or terminal illness, also may greatly affect how successfully and quickly we recover from our loss. Deaths from suicide, homicide, and accident are especially painful for families to experience and process. Deaths such as these have the potential for dysfunctional mourning because of the violence of the death and the shock of the loss—sudden deaths being more traumatic emotionally. If severe trauma occurred to the body, preventing viewing prior to burial, the bereaved may have difficulty accomplishing the first task of mourning. Viewing any part of the body, clothing, or personal possessions worn at the time of death may help survivors accept that the individual is actually dead.

Suicide

Suicidal deaths frequently invoke feelings of shame, guilt, and anger in survivors. Depression is common in people grieving suicides, as they dwell on what might have been done to prevent the death. Some views of suicide promote social isolation of the bereaved when a suicide occurs. If the suicide is not acknowledged, the family won't have their pain validated, making recovery more difficult. The case of Mike's sister Kathy is a good example of how we react to suicide in our society.

When Mike was 18, his older sister Kathy, an intensive-care nurse, committed suicide by a self-inflicted bullet wound. Family and friends were shocked and dismayed at her death. Kathy's suicide note made her motivation clear—she had been diagnosed with terminal cancer and killed herself to spare her family the expense and trauma of her otherwise slow, agonizing death. Kathy's family was not ashamed of her suicide or reluctant to talk about it. For some of their neighbors and relatives it was a different story. Even when told by Kathy's family that suicide was the cause of death, some people refused to accept it, saying that her death must have been accidental.

Homicide

Homicide may invoke intense feelings of rage in the bereaved. Although the bereaved may be able to channel their strong feelings toward seeking justice through the legal system, the courts move slowly and justice is not always served from the point of view of the bereaved family. Intense feelings of anger may remain focused and unreleased, or they may be displaced to other family members, co-workers, teachers, or classmates.

Homicidal deaths are especially likely to result in chronic grief reactions in survivors, as they become "secondary victims" of the media, medical personnel, and the criminal justice system. Every time another hearing is held, the bereaved must go through the trauma of the death experience all over again. Survivors come face to face with the murder suspect every time they enter the courtroom. If the murderer is not identified and the circumstances of the death go unresolved, survivors may compulsively review events in search of answers to why and how the death occurred.

Accidents

Accidents are the number one cause of death in youth and children. These deaths may be particularly traumatic to witness. Witnesses may repeatedly flash the scene of the accident through their minds, each time also re-experiencing the trauma. This is called "death imprinting." The following case is a good example.

Four boys were riding their bikes one afternoon. One challenged the others to a race down a steep hill. One boy lost control of his bicycle and rammed into a tree. He died instantly of a broken neck. Ever since, the three surviving boys have suffered from anxiety, flashbacks, and nightmares. All three have been referred to private therapy.

Terminal Illness

Death following a terminal illness results in a very different kind of grief because there is some forewarning that death is imminent. This provides the opportunity to process many feelings, to attend to unfinished business, and experience anticipatory grief. During the final stages of the illness, roles and responsibilities performed by the terminally ill person may be shifted to other family members. Loved ones have time to make amends for any wrong-doing and to express their love and appreciation for one another. This is a time when life frequently is lived in the present moment and priorities are clarified.

This doesn't make dying from a terminal illness easy, however. Experiencing the last weeks, days, and hours of life for someone, especially a child, who is dying of a terminal illness may be more emotionally painful and stressful for survivors than the death itself. It's common to want to conceal the poor prognosis from the ill person to protect him or her from further pain and anxiety, but this should be avoided. The terminally ill person is likely to suspect that death is imminent and feel fearful, anxious, angry, and sad. Without validation of these feelings by loved ones, the ill person won't get the emotional support necessary to face death. The terminally ill need to be able to talk about dying, finish unfinished business, and go through the stages of acceptance of death. Refer to Chapter 10, Lesson 4 in *Glencoe Health*. This doesn't mean that the terminally ill should be focused only on death. In fact, they need to feel that they are alive until the moment of death by being given every opportunity to live life as normally and as fully as their illness permits. The

family and friends of the dying person also must cope with death. Grief and mourning can develop through a series of stages much like stages of dying.

Teens and Death

Child development experts believe that sometime between ages 9 and 12, most children begin to recognize and accept that death is permanent, universal to all living things, and will happen to them some day. Yet despite their mature comprehension of death, teens experience and process loss differently than adults do for several reasons.

Teens are experiencing massive social, emotional, and physical changes in their lives as they work their way through adolescence, so they may be more severely affected by the added stress of death and bereavement than adults are. The death of a close friend, sibling, parent, or teacher changes interpersonal relationships at a time when identities and roles are already ambiguous.

Teens lack the perspective of years and experience that teaches us that even intense emotional pain can lessen. As a consequence, they tend to have more difficulty dealing with grief than do adults. This lengthens the time it takes teens to work through their feelings and complete the stages of mourning. Storing away unfinished grief each time a loss occurs may lead to overload, even if the losses are not due to death but events like moving to a new town, school failure, or divorce. Teens who have experienced many such losses are described as "grief prone." Any additional loss in a grief-prone individual has the capacity to become the "straw that broke the camel's back," triggering a resurgence of earlier feelings and memories of loss.

Loss of self-esteem has been observed in all bereaved persons, but teens tend to have less stability in their sense of self and self-worth, so they are especially at risk of developing poor self-esteem and in need of confirmation of their worth. Loss of a parent, in particular, can have a negative impact on self-esteem because death represents the ultimate abandonment. The bereaved teen may believe he or she is unlovable and may develop long-term problems with self-esteem. Feelings of ambivalence toward either parent—the deceased or the survivor—can lead to intense feelings of guilt, blame, hostility, or regret.

A parent's death in early adolescence frequently leads to a regression to less mature behavior. Young teens may become more dependent and need more attention just when other family members are preoccupied with their own grief. When older teens experience the death of a parent, they may be forced into a surrogate parent role. Then, several outcomes are possible, ranging from acquiescence—at the expense of their few remaining years of youthful irresponsibility—to running away from home to escape the burdens thrust upon them. Roles and responsibilities within the family need to be adjusted, but replacement of the parental role through a child is unhealthy. Few teens are ready to take on adult responsibilities before they have finished their own growth and development.

Good communication, especially of feelings, is critical to the healthy resolution of loss. Unfortunately, intergenerational communication problems between teens and their parents are legion. These may be exacerbated following a major loss, as family members are suffering through different stages of mourning the death. The support of peers, with whom communication is easier, may become very important. On the other hand, teens who haven't experienced a loss and are concerned about mundane things like clothes and grades, may seem immature to teens who are focused on the loss of a loved one and their own grief. It's not surprising that social isolation and loss of interest in extra-curricular activities are common in bereaved teens.

Death of a school employee, particularly a favorite teacher, may parallel the loss of a parent to some students. Other students may not have had such a close relationship with the deceased and may be less affected. Some may even feel relief that the individual is no longer around. This may lead to feelings of guilt and shame. Death by suicide of a school employee may be particularly difficult to accept. Students may question how they can be expected to cope successfully with life's problems if a respected adult cannot. If a fellow student dies, other students may be triggered to experience strong feelings during school events they shared with the deceased. If the death was by suicide, parents and school staff may be tempted to suppress information regarding the cause of death for fear of "copy-cat" suicides, failing to realize that correct information about the death is necessary so survivors can accept the death, process the loss, and complete the tasks of mourning.

The more mature and experienced teenagers are in grieving losses, the greater the likelihood that they'll successfully recover from the emotional pain of a death. Good emotional support, to help teens accept the death and process the feelings of loss, also promotes successful recovery. Families in which the surviving parents can't provide the needed emotional support to their children may need outside help. With a support system outside the family, teens who have experienced loss, emotional neglect, and even abandonment within their families are much more likely to recover successfully from their grief. The availability of same-sex role models, for example, through extended family, friends, or school professionals, can help mitigate feelings of abandonment and poor self-esteem. Clearly, teachers, school counselors, and other school personnel may play significant roles in the recovery of teens from the emotional pain of a death. The next two chapters describe in detail how schools and teachers can help in the recovery process.

CHAPTER 2

HOW SCHOOLS CAN HELP

The purpose of this chapter is to describe support services schools can provide to bereaved students. As a teacher, you may have little to say about whether or not your school provides the services, but if it does, you can become involved in them and encourage students to become involved in them, too.

Schools Need to Help

Although the family is, ideally, the primary source of emotional support for bereaved teens, many grieving families are unable to provide the extra nurturing their members need. As a result, emotional support to help grieving teens through their mourning often must come from outside the family. For many students, the only other potential source of support is their school, including teachers, other staff, and classmates. This is especially likely for students living in homes where abuse or neglect prevail. While such students may need professional counseling, they also need confirmation of their worth and opportunities to achieve success, and those are needs that the school can meet. The support such students get at school may serve as an important buffer to the distress they may be experiencing at home.

Quite understandably, some who are reading this book may not feel qualified to help students who are suffering great emotional pain. They may feel overwhelmed by a student's need for emotional support when their own time and energy are stretched thin by the demands of job and family. They're far from alone if they feel uncomfortable dealing with death, particularly by being reminded that it will ultimately affect them and those they love. Most readers would no doubt agree that the schools have a hard enough time just teaching knowledge and skills, without being expected to provide emotional support to

grieving students. Unfortunately, most students who are grieving can't put aside emotional pain when they're at school. If the school is to provide a learning environment for them, bereaved students must be able to attain emotional health after experiencing a loss. Clearly, schools must do what they can to help grieving students recover from their emotional pain.

What Schools Can Do

Ideally, most school personnel, and especially those with close student contact, should be provided with professional inservice training in how to respond positively to death and support the recovery of grieving students, while continuing to achieve educational goals. Students also should be taught about death and dying, including how to mourn a loss, through teaching strategies that can be incorporated into the regular curriculum. Then, students can help each other during times of bereavement.

Establish a Response Team

Every school should have a plan in place for responding to an immediate crisis of a death, like the traumatic event response team described later in this chapter. Every school also should provide longer-term solutions for the bereaved, including peer support groups (discussed in this chapter), referrals to professional help (see Chapter 3), and a classroom environment that encourages healing and the development of grief-recovery skills (also in Chapter 3).

The major purpose of a traumatic event response team is to respond to the death of a staff member or student by providing immediate support to anyone in the school environment in need of assistance with the grief process. The team may also assist teachers or students in responding to suicide attempts, death or terminal illness of students' family members, and community tragedies that affect students and school staff.

The overall goal of the response team should be to facilitate order, calm, and grief recovery during a crisis. The members of the team should be charged with developing guidelines to be followed by the school when any kind of crisis occurs. The guidelines should be specific regarding the roles and responsibilities of each team member. It's very important that a single individual is designated as responsible for collecting information regarding the event and for developing announcements to be made to parents, teachers, students, and the media. This role is usually assigned to the principal. All communication should flow in and out of the school system through the designated contact person. A team coordinator also should be identified. Often this role is filled by the school counselor. Alternates should be assigned for all roles on the team.

In addition to the principal and school counselor, appropriate persons to participate in the response team are the school nurse, teachers, and informed community members, such as mental health counselors, hospice staff, and death educators from local universities. Members of the clergy and funeral directors may also be relevant team members, especially if they have received special training in death education and counseling. Teachers selected to serve on the team should be volunteers—they're more likely to have experienced and grieved a significant loss and therefore to be aware of the needs of bereaved students. All members of the team should be comfortable dealing with the subject of death. No one should be required to serve on the team, regardless of their academic or professional preparation, if they feel uncomfortable doing so.

Once the team has been identified, inservice training should be provided, if needed, in grief responses and how to facilitate mourning. Local mental health professionals, hospice programs, and educators certified by the Association of Death Educators and Counselors may assist with teacher training. Many state departments of education also have professionals who can provide such inservice training. In addition to training, members of the response team need to:

- work through their own feelings about previous losses;
- be comfortable with all types of deaths;
- be able to remain calm during a crisis.

Many traumatic event response teams are being established today in schools in which a tragedy occurred that the school was unprepared to handle. Ideally, the team should be organized and trained prior to a tragic event.

Inform Students of the Death

It's extremely important that students be given accurate, factual information about a death. This helps dispel rumors and promotes acceptance of the fact of the death. Either the principal or school counselor should be responsible for gathering specifics of the death and preparing a statement to be shared in small groups such as in homerooms by homeroom teachers. Announcements over the intercom or in large assemblies of students should be avoided. Care should be taken not to imply that the deceased was responsible for his or her own death through risky behavior, such as the use of drugs.

At the very least, the school should be prepared to give students:

- accurate and appropriate information about the death;
- opportunities to share their feelings;
- opportunities to mourn and activities to honor the deceased;
- encouragement to participate in life.

Share Feelings

Sharing the information in the security of a classroom among a small group of peers gives students the opportunity to ask questions and talk about their feelings. Homeroom teachers should pay special attention to students who had a close relationship with the deceased. These students may need to be able to talk through their feelings with responsive individuals or with other students in small groups. If another teacher has a good rapport with a particular student, his or her help should be elicited. For students who are particularly emotional over the death, a "quiet" room should be available where they can release feelings and get temporary emotional support.

Mourn for and Honor the Deceased

Giving students opportunities to mourn is a healthy way to facilitate their experiences in the tasks of mourning. Students may participate in the funeral as pallbearers, or take part in a musical tribute.

There are many different activities students may participate in to honor the deceased. More importantly for the bereaved, such activities also provide a healthy catharsis of feelings. Students can collect money to purchase live plants or trees, which can be placed in the school or planted on the school grounds in honor of the deceased. A special plaque honoring the deceased may be designed and placed in the school. The school yearbook or newspaper may have a special memorial section honoring the deceased. If the deceased participated in sports, a moment of silence may be held at a sporting event. A plaque may be given to the family at an awards banquet, or the deceased's number might be retired. A scholarship fund may be established in honor of the deceased. Graduation services may include special mention of the deceased.

Although we tend to downplay deaths by suicide, it's equally important to commemorate a death by suicide. Consider the following case.

A high school chose to ignore the self-inflicted gunshot death of a popular student. The students expressed their need to remember her during graduation ceremonies. They asked that her name be called, with a moment of silence in her honor. The principal refused. During graduation, the students deliberately left an empty seat and placed a rose where, alphabetically, the deceased would have been seated. They clearly expressed their need to remember and to honor her.

Encourage Participation in Life

Bereaved individuals tend to withdraw from their usual activities in order to reduce additional stimulation. It's a natural, protective reaction. However, reinvesting in life is important for recovery to be complete. Bereaved students need to be given encouragement from teachers, staff, and classmates to participate in school-related activities.

It's important to realize that some students will not recover to the point of functioning normally for months. Others severely affected by a death may experience problems for years. The differing responses of the bereaved should be acknowledged and validated.

Set up Support Groups

The purpose of a support group is to facilitate the recovery of students who are especially affected by a death. A support group is not intended as a therapy group, but as an opportunity for extended emotional support and guidance for students who need additional time to process their feelings. Students perceived to be in need of professional help should be screened out of the support group from the beginning and given the proper referral. Students who have unresolved previous losses, who are involved in abusive family situations, or who, for various reasons, have been severely affected by the death, are best served by a counselor or therapist who can provide professional care.

Guidelines for referral to a support group should be developed by the traumatic event response team or by a bereavement specialist. Membership in the group should not exceed ten students. If a larger number of students need to join a group, another support group should be formed. Groups should be closed to new members once formed, and the membership should remain as stable as possible. Participation in the support group should be voluntary, but once students make a commitment to the group, they should be encouraged to participate for the duration of the scheduled time. Support groups normally meet for up to ten weeks. Group meetings can be held during study halls or after school.

Group leaders should be identified and, if necessary, trained in group process as well as activities beneficial to the bereaved. Counselors, psychologists, and social workers employed by the school are appropriate support group leaders. Professionals from the mental health or hospice community also may facilitate support groups.

Co-leaders are recommended for support groups so that the responsibilities of leading the group can be shared. Co-leaders ensure that a group leader will be available in case of a conflict or illness. In addition, having two leaders allows one person to lead activities while the other observes student reactions. At the end of each session, the co-leaders can discuss what happened in the group and identify issues that need to be addressed in future sessions.

The first session should begin with the students introducing themselves to the group. (Because distraught students may not remember the names of other members, it may be necessary to repeat introductions at subsequent sessions.) Ground rules should be clearly established at this time. These should include confidentiality, permission to speak and express feelings freely, as well as permission to pass if students aren't ready to express their feelings. Students should be encouraged to share their experiences with regard to the death, including how they felt when they first heard about the death and how they feel now. This will help the group leader(s) identify issues to deal with in future sessions and provide an opportunity to assure students that their feelings are normal.

Before the end of the first session, activities that students will take part in in upcoming sessions should be discussed so that students know what lies ahead. (Appropriate activities can be selected from the teaching strategies described in Chapter 4.) The tasks of mourning should also be described so students will know the path they must follow to recover from their grief.

Closure of the first and subsequent sessions should include a summary of what occurred in the session, confirmation of the students as valuable human beings who are suffering from emotional pain, and assurance that their pain is real but can be overcome.

Teachers, counselors, librarians, secretaries, bus drivers, and other school personnel may be among the bereaved, and they may need opportunities to meet in small groups to discuss the death and share their feelings. This may be done informally, or a structured session may be scheduled for the end of the first day and any day thereafter, as long as there is a need. Small group discussions also facilitate communication among school professionals regarding the status of particular students' grief recovery.

The Case of Franklin High

The following story of how one high school responded to the accidental death of a student provides a good model for other schools to follow. Because Franklin High had a traumatic event response team in place, it was able to deal quickly and effectively with the tragedy.

Remember Roy? He's the boy who was struck by a car while crossing the road after getting off the school bus. Many of his friends and classmates from Franklin High School witnessed the tragedy. Their screams filled the bus as they saw Roy's limp body being dragged down the road by the car.

Franklin High's principal, Evelyn Smith, got the call from the police on the scene. There was no doubt of the fact of Roy's death—it could be announced as soon as Roy's parents had been contacted. Principal Smith felt special concern for the 30 or so students who witnessed Roy's death—and the other 1200 plus students at Franklin High.

The shock and horror of the accident and its senselessness would make resolution of the death and the ensuing grief much more difficult.

Principal Smith was glad that the school had formed a traumatic event response team last year. By this time, all team members had been assigned specific roles, with alternates for each position, and they'd all received inservice training in death and grief. The rest of the staff and teachers had been given written instructions describing the general plan the response team had drawn up for dealing with emergencies, such as Roy's death. In it, the roles of teachers and other staff were clearly spelled out. This was the first time all of them would be tested by an actual traumatic event.

When Principal Smith was sure she had the correct facts regarding the death, she put into place the telephone relay system that was part of the overall plan. She called two people on the team directly—the school counselor and the school nurse, co-coordinators of the traumatic event response team. The counselor and nurse each called two others, who in turn called two others. This continued until all members had been called. In less than 20 minutes, all but one of the 12 members of the response team had been contacted. The information conveyed over the phone was kept brief and to-the-point to prevent errors in communication and to expedite a face-to-face meeting of team members. The meeting was held that evening at the school. Team members fine-tuned the general plan for the situation at hand and notified the rest of the staff of a meeting before school the next morning.

Next morning, at the beginning of the meeting, Principal Smith gave everyone a written statement describing the details of Roy's death to be read in their homeroom classes when school started. She also passed out written information regarding changes in scheduling of classes, exams, and extra-curricular activities for the rest of the day. Any further schedule changes would be given to the staff as soon as they were available. Details of the wake and funeral would also follow.

Then, response team members took over. First, they reviewed the guidelines for identifying students who needed referral to a "quiet" room staffed by team members, to a support group, or to individual counseling. Checklists were passed out to aid teachers in identifying which students needed each type of referral. The response team also gave the staff a list of community resources for long-term follow-up and bereavement care.

In addition to the information they received, the staff was given the opportunity to express their own feelings and recover from the initial shock prior to meeting with students.

Back in their homerooms, Franklin High's teachers prepared themselves for the arrival of their students. Many of those present looked distraught, and many appeared to be on the verge of tears. In each class, the homeroom teacher read the statement prepared by Principal Smith describing Roy's death. Some of the teachers didn't feel capable of discussing the accident with students alone, so response team members were there to assist them. Team members also assisted the teacher in Roy's homeroom class. Students who were Roy's close friends and who were likely to be most affected by the death had been identified by the response team so that extra support would be available to them immediately.

Throughout the rest of that first day, an effort was made to maintain the basic class schedule and school routine as much as possible. Response team members kept themselves highly visible and could be identified by name tags. Teachers informed students that team members were there to help them and encouraged students to ask team members for support if they felt they needed it.

Support was given to several students who spent time in the quiet room, staffed by response team members. Here they were encouraged to express their feelings, by crying or talking about Roy, before returning to class. Ten students were referred to the school counselor, who met with them individually and later that day in an informal support group. Three of these students were referred to individual counseling. Parents of students who continued to have difficulty calming down were contacted and asked to pick the students up at school if possible. Distraught students weren't allowed to leave the school without an adult or to go home without a parent or other adult there to greet and support them.

By the next morning, Principal Smith had the details on the wake and funeral, including how students could be involved. She had also received permission from Roy's family to plan memorials in his honor. She had contacted the funeral home to see how many students they could accommodate at one time. She prepared and distributed a statement for homeroom teachers to read explaining opportunities for students to participate in the wake and funeral. No one was pressured to participate. The number of students planning to attend was determined and relayed to the principal so she could prepare the funeral home and family for the students' arrival.

Students in Roy's class were asked if there was anything special they would like to do to honor Roy's death. Several suggestions were made, including: holding a school memorial service; starting a scholarship fund in Roy's name; dedicating the school play, in which Roy had a small part, to his memory; and planting a tree on the school grounds with a plaque bearing Roy's name. All suggestions were given to Principal Smith who, in turn, relayed them to Roy's family for their approval.

Later that day, Principal Smith and other members of the response team arranged for flowers, food, cards, and letters from students and staff to be sent to Roy's family or the funeral home. They also decided when the school flag was to be lowered, for how long, and who would be responsible for doing it. They cleared Roy's personal effects from the school and delivered them to his family.

During the rest of the week, a school memorial service was planned by student volunteers and response team members. Students were given roles to play in the service, and response team members were present to assist.

Principal Smith knew that the mourning of Roy's death had only just begun for Roy's closest friends. Students who had witnessed the accident might need extended counseling. Because of the advance planning of the response team, those students had been identified early and had received appropriate attention from the start. Principal Smith knew that the school, its staff, and its students had handled a major traumatic event quickly, efficiently, and humanely. Things were more or less back to normal, but Roy's memory would live on in the memorials that were planned to honor him.

CHAPTER 3

WHAT TEACHERS CAN DO

The purpose of this chapter is to offer suggestions concerning ways that teachers can help students recover from grief. Although the primary role of a teacher working with bereaved students is to educate them, it is important to remember that the bereaved are working through their grief and that grief is emotionally and physically exhausting work. Understanding and respecting bereaved students' needs and emotions is critical to facilitating learning as well as to supporting mourning.

The case of Jeremy shows how educational aims can be thwarted if the emotional needs of bereaved students are disregarded.

Jeremy's younger sister died of leukemia. His English teacher was very insensitive to his grief. When Jeremy drifted off into thinking about his sister, her death, or the funeral, the teacher criticized him for daydreaming and badgered him to get back to work. Jeremy had no motivation to do his English homework. Jeremy failed English that year.

The same year Jeremy had a history teacher who was very attuned to Jeremy's grief because his own mother had died the previous year. He knew what Jeremy was experiencing and gave him extra time and other considerations in his class work. He also helped Jeremy work through his grief by encouraging him to talk about his sister and her death. Jeremy got an A in history that year.

Help Bereaved Students

From this example, it is clear that bereaved students may have great difficulty returning to the normal routines of school. They may suffer loss of emotional control, have difficulty concentrat-ing, be subject to daydreaming, have sleep problems, and suffer from fatigue. Students who are severely affected by a loss may have little motivation for doing their school work as they attempt to sort through what life is all about. Self-esteem may decline when a student receives lower grades than he or she usually gets.

Increased health problems also may contribute to the difficulty bereaved students have with their school work. Extreme emotional stress may lower their resistance, making them prone to a variety of ailments, including headaches, stomach aches, diarrhea, rashes, and viral infections such as colds.

Clearly, bereaved students should be given special consideration. Extended deadlines, make-up exams, and tutoring are ways teachers can help bereaved students cope with grief and school work at the same time.

Any opportunity given to bereaved students to express their feelings will help them work through their grief. The classroom environment should be open to questions about the death and discussion of the deceased. Bereaved students should be encouraged to recall positive memories as well as to share the pain of the loss. To help facilitate sharing of feelings and to teach students more about feelings of loss, use Activities 1 to 7 in Chapter 4.

The most common emotion felt early in the grief process is sadness, usually expressed through crying. If students begin to cry, you can give them tacit permission to express their feelings this way by simply handing them a tissue without comment. Speaking to the student may disrupt the release of feelings. If you feel comfortable expressing your own feelings, it gives bereaved students permission to express theirs. You also validate their feelings by sharing your own.

Students who are experiencing feelings of anger and powerlessness over a death can be encouraged to find healthy outlets for their anger. Survivors of homicides might get involved in lobbying for handgun control legislation. Students who have lost loved ones in alcohol-related car crashes can join Students Against Driving Drunk (SADD). Those who have lost family members or friends to cancer might do volunteer work for the American Cancer Society or at a local hospital. Involving bereaved students in decision-making regarding classroom activities also can foster a sense of power and control.

While it's often helpful to get the bereaved involved in activities, be aware of activities that were once shared with the deceased. Such activities may be too painful to pursue because they remind the bereaved too much of their loss. Consider the following example:

> *The football coach recognized that John had the physical potential to be a good player and asked him on several occasions to join the team. Finally, John stayed after school to watch the other students practice. He came home feeling depressed. He was reminded of the last day he spent with his deceased brother. The final experience John had shared with him was a game of touch football. After several days, John stayed after school to watch practice again. Finally, he decided to join the team. He went to practice a few times, but it always brought back strong feelings of loss of his brother. After a few weeks, John withdrew from the team.*

Teach Other Classmates to Be Supportive

During adolescence, peers play an increasingly significant role. Small group activities and peer tutoring among bereaved teens or teens who have suffered any sort of loss can promote peer support. Such cooperative learning experiences may facilitate the sharing of grief experiences and the realization that loss and grieving are universal.

Students who haven't experienced a loss need to learn how to be supportive of their bereaved classmates. Activities 3 and 4 and 9 to 11 in Chapter 4 will help them learn how to listen to feelings and to provide emotional support. The listening skills discussed later in this chapter also can help students become better listeners.

While the bereaved should be encouraged to talk about the death and their grief, classmates may sometimes become overzealous and start probing too much. Sometimes, too, behavior of bereaved students may lead to gossip, rumors, or teasing by classmates. Making classmates aware

of the insensitivity of their behavior may be all that's needed to prevent it.

Become Better Listeners

One of the most important ways to support the bereaved and help them successfully recover from their loss is to listen to and validate their feelings. Teachers and classmates of bereaved students can use the following guidelines to become better listeners:

- Pay close attention to nonverbal communication as well as to the bereaved's words. Observe facial expressions, gestures, and posture.
- Listen to the feelings that underlie the words. Don't just listen to the facts.
- Really listen. Don't just pretend to listen while your mind wanders off to other subjects.
- Don't interject your own stories of loss but stay focused on the bereaved's experience.
- Use paraphrasing or reflective listening techniques to assure the bereaved that you are truly listening.
- Maximize the use of nonverbal skills to communicate empathy by your tone of voice, eye contact, and touch.
- Accept the bereaved's feelings and adopt a nonjudgmental attitude. Assume the position that the feelings are normal and neither right nor wrong. Avoid advising, warning, criticizing, or questioning the bereaved.
- Don't attempt to resolve the bereaved's grief, but project a belief in his or her ability to resolve the feelings.
- Respect the bereaved's confidence by not sharing private information with others.
- Create opportunities to be with the bereaved to talk about the loss. Encourage participation in discussions, seek his or her opinions, and offer praise for ways responsibilities were handled.

Recognize When Professional Help Is Needed

One of the most important responsibilities teachers have toward bereaved students is monitoring them and referring them to the school counselor if they think professional help may be needed. Teachers usually see their students on a daily basis, so they are most likely to notice signs or symptoms of dysfunctional grieving in students. Students who show no emotion and mourn silently may be in greater danger because of their inability to release feelings. Teens who exhibit any of the signs or symptoms of dysfunctional grieving that were discussed in Chapter 1 should be referred to the school counselor or psychologist. School counselors can make referrals to other counselors or clergy who can ensure that appropriate help is obtained. Teens who have experienced a major loss, such as a parent, sibling, or best friend, may need help for as much as two years.

It is helpful to know which students might be at risk of dysfunctional grieving. Several factors have been associated with higher risk, including:

- lack of support for the loss at home or school;
- a loss that occurs before age five or during early adolescence;
- loss of a mother by girls before adolescence and loss of a father by boys during adolescence;
- pre-existing psychological problems;
- conflicts in the relationship with the deceased;
- an emotionally distraught surviving parent who is overly dependent on the bereaved teen;
- an unstable past environment that involved changes in caretakers, moves to new locations, or other disruptions in family routines;
- a negative relationship between the teen and a parental replacement figure;
- lack of previous experience with death or loss;
- unexpected or traumatic death, such as by homicide or suicide, especially of a sibling or parent.

Help Those Who Are Anticipating Grief

Students in class who have terminally ill loved ones are in a unique position. They may already be experiencing anticipatory grief, yet are expected to continue with school as usual. Be aware that students with terminally ill loved ones may not be able to perform in school or interact with others as usual. Additional assistance and support for them may be needed.

Be Aware of Symptoms of Suicide

Suicide is of special concern to those who work closely with teens because of the high rates of teen suicide. The following may be warning signs of suicide:

- a previous suicide attempt;
- threats or talk of suicide;
- a pattern of self-destructive behavior, such as risk-taking with an automobile or drugs;
- loss of interest in life;
- loss of appetite or weight;
- calm behavior after a period of conflict or depression;
- giving away possessions, making amends, or saying good-bye to loved ones;
- developing a plan or obtaining the means to commit suicide;
- written or other creative works that show repeated themes of depression, pressure, or death;
- a sudden change in any pattern of behavior.

If a bereaved student shows any of the warning signs of suicide, he or she should be referred to professional help immediately. If you suspect a bereaved student may be suicidal even though no warning signs have been observed, ask the student if he or she is considering hurting himself or herself and ask if this is the worst things have been. If the answer is yes to either question, refer the student to the school counselor immediately. In addition, you should:

- always take a suicidal person seriously—never discount or dismiss a threat;
- remain calm—don't express shock or try to challenge the person;
- assure the person that he or she can cope and must live with the problems at hand but don't try to minimize the problems;
- never play therapist but always be caring, supportive, and concerned;
- never agree to "keep the secret";
- be firm with the person that something must be done—if necessary, offer to take action because the individual may feel so hopeless and helpless that he or she cannot act in his or her own best interest;
- never argue the pros and cons of suicide;
- never assume that the person will be okay tomorrow or in a few days.

STRATEGIES AND ACTIVITIES FOR GRIEF RECOVERY

The purpose of this chapter is to provide activities to help students develop the skills they need to grieve a loss successfully. These include activities related to stress reduction, life-management skills, communication, decision making, and conflict resolution. For further information, refer students to several relevant sections in the *Glencoe Health* text such as Lesson 4 in Chapter 10. You also can encourage students to look up related subjects in the library. Suggested resources are listed in the Appendix of this book.

The activities that follow can be integrated into Art, Music, and Language Arts classes, in addition to Health Education classes. Some offer cooperative learning experiences and others offer opportunities for thought-provoking private reflection. Students should never feel pressured to participate in the activities. You might choose to describe the activities to the class and ask them which ones they feel most comfortable with. Encourage participation in activities that can provide success and support to counter a person's loss of self-esteem that is normal following the death of a friend or loved one.

Objectives

The objectives of the following activities are to aid the student in expressing his or her feelings in order to recover from the death of a friend or family member.

Students will:
- become aware that we all experience loss and grief in our lifetimes;
- have the opportunity to express their feelings over a loss in their lives and share their feelings with others;
- by acknowledging and sharing their feelings over a loss, begin to work through their grief;

- improve their ability to "listen" to others' feelings associated with loss;
- increase their awareness of the variety of feelings we may experience with a loss;
- be reassured that feelings of grief are normal;
- have an opportunity to say things they needed to say to the deceased, including good-bye;
- increase their awareness of the need for support during a loss;
- identify who is included in their personal support systems.

Activity: Dealing With Loss

Ask students to think back through their lives to an event that represented a loss to them. Emphasize that the event does not have to be the death of a person. It could be a best friend moving away, a home destroyed, the death of a pet, divorce of parents, a parent losing a job, a bankruptcy, or any other loss. Have them close their eyes and try to visualize how it was to go through that time in their lives. Ask students to write a brief description of how they felt and how their lives changed because of the loss. Have them describe how they were treated by others and how they wish they had been treated. Tell them they don't need to reveal the nature of the loss in their descriptions.

Divide the class into small groups and ask for volunteers to share their paragraphs. If no one feels comfortable sharing their loss with others, explain that expressing their feelings on paper is also cathartic.

Activity: The Life Continuum

Ask students to draw a line on a sheet of paper. Explain to the class that the line represents their lives as a continuum, with one end representing birth and the other end representing death. Ask them to place a mark on the continuum that shows where they are now. Ask them to go back to their birth and come forward in time, making a mark and listing the age at which they experienced any type of loss. Ask them to write a brief description of each loss, how they felt at the time, and how the loss affected their lives.

Activity: Listen/Communicate

Ask students to think about how people act when they're not really listening to another person. For example, they may be reading the newspaper, watching television, filing their nails, or doing some other distracting activity while the speaker is talking. They may interrupt, change the subject, or begin to share a personal story about something similar that happened to them.

Group about half the students in the class into pairs. In each pair, assign one student the role of listener and one the role of communicator. Instruct the communicators to describe a real or hypothetical emotion-laden situation. Ask about half of the listeners to really listen to what the communicator in the pair is saying—not just the details of the situation but feelings as well. Ask the rest of the listeners to just pretend to listen or listen only halfheartedly while doing something else. The unpaired members of the class should try to identify which students were asked to listen and which were asked to just pretend to listen. Have the class take notes on what behaviors helped them differentiate the two types of listeners (e.g., doing something else, showing inappropriate facial expressions). Ask the communicators to describe how they felt when the other people did and did not listen.

Activity: Facts and Feelings

Divide the class into several small groups. Ask for a volunteer in each group to share a loss, real or hypothetical, with the others. Ask some of the remaining group members to listen to the facts and the rest to listen to the feelings the volunteer is expressing. After the volunteer has finished describing the loss, ask the listeners to share their perceptions. The volunteer should clarify any misconceptions of the listeners and contrast any differences between the two types of listeners that he or she observed or sensed. Have the groups discuss how listening for feelings differs from listening for facts.

Activity: Fill in the Blanks

This activity is applicable to a recent death experience shared by members of the class. Have students write the numbers 1 to 9 on a sheet of paper. Read the following sentences to them and ask them to complete each sentence in their own words, recording their answers on the paper. Assure students that there are no right or wrong answers and that they won't have to share what they write with anyone unless they wish to. After the exercise is completed, ask for volunteers to share their responses. If no one wishes to volunteer, share with the class some of the possible responses given in brackets or come up with some of your own. Generate class discussion about the responses (e.g., How widely do they vary? Which ones are similar or shared by many?).

1. Death is [*scary, cruel, a joke, inevitable, certain...*].
2. Talking about death is [*hard, scary, embarrassing, thought-provoking, unburdening...*].
3. I am (not) afraid of death because [*it's unknown, I love life, it's unfair, I'm afraid of what awaits me after death, I believe in a better afterlife, I'm at peace with myself...*].
4. When [*name of deceased*] died, I felt [*shocked, numb, overwhelmed, in disbelief...*].
5. When I think about the funeral, I feel [*sad, emotional, empty, released...*].
6. Now when I think of [*name of deceased*], I feel [*sad, angry, resentful, regretful, guilty, ashamed...*].
7. One thing I regret when I think of [*name of deceased*] is [*not telling him/her how I felt about him/her; not making up after a fight; his/her lost future; his/her presence in class or on the team...*].
8. If I could tell [*name of deceased*] one thing, I would say [*I love you, I miss you, you hurt me, you should have done things differently...*].
9. If I could ask [*name of deceased*] one thing, I would ask [*Did you love me? Do you forgive me? Why did you abandon me? What is death?*]

Activity: Unfinished Business

This activity is applicable to a recent death experience shared by members of the class. Have students work individually to write letters to the deceased to resolve any unfinished business between them. Suggestions for what might be addressed in the letters include: things they wish they'd said or done; things they regret saying or doing; things they need to have forgiven; things they'd like to say right now if they could; things they wish they could ask; the way they might say good-bye. If any students wish to volunteer to share their letters or parts of their letters with the rest of the class, encourage them to do so. Tell students that the expression of their feelings and the resolution of their unfinished business will help them accept the death and recover from their grief.

Activity: Expressing Feelings

Give a piece of chalk to the first person sitting in each row. Have them go to the chalkboard and write one feeling they have experienced following a loss. After they've written a feeling on the board, they should pass the chalk to the next person in the row. If any student had thought of the same feeling or emotion as one already on the chalkboard, he or she should put a check mark by the word. Assure students that they may pass if they wish. After all students who wish to participate have had the opportunity to write a feeling on the chalkboard, comment on which feelings were most often shared. Point out that we all have many of the same feelings even though the nature of our losses may be different. Remind students of the importance of acknowledging and expressing feelings in recovering from grief.

Objectives

The objectives of the following activities are to give students the opportunities to learn how to help when others are grieving.

Students will:
- learn to speak with the bereaved in a way that helps instead of hurts;
- get practice in interacting with bereaved individuals;
- get insights into how they would feel if they were bereaved;
- be given an opportunity to share their feelings about the deceased with the bereaved family.

Activity: Helping Qualities

Ask students to write down whom they would turn to if they experienced a loss. Suggest that the list might include their parents, close friends, and relatives. Then, ask them to identify what they consider to be the most positive, helping qualities of each person named. Ask students to think about their own qualities and how they might provide support to a friend who is bereaved.

Activity: Dos and Don'ts

Write two headings on the chalkboard: "What to Say" and "What Not to Say." Ask students to brainstorm what they might say to someone grieving a significant loss when they see him or her for the first time after the loss occurred. Ask students to suggest a greeting and follow-up comments or topics of conversation. Ask them to decide if the statements are "Dos" or "Don'ts" and list them in the appropriate columns. For "Don't" entries, ask students why the comment or topic is a "Don't" and how it could be changed to make it more acceptable. Ask for volunteers to role-play the greetings and comments with another student who assumes the role of the bereaved.

Activity: Comfort Zone

Ask students to brainstorm why they think many people are uncomfortable around a bereaved person. List the reasons on the chalkboard. Then ask students what they think they could do to become more comfortable with the bereaved. Finally, ask them how they would like to be treated if they were bereaved.

Activity: Sympathy/Empathy

Point out that bereaved people derive little, if any, benefit from our sympathy. Ask students the difference between sympathy and empathy. (Sympathy is sharing common feelings and emotions with another person. Empathy is understanding and participating in another person's feelings and emotions.) Then have them work individually or in groups to write an empathetic letter to a bereaved family. Suggest that they include special memories and what they miss most about the deceased.

APPENDIX

RESOURCES

The following is a list of organizations and book titles for further information and assistance as you work with bereaved teens.

Organizations

AMEND (Aiding Mothers and Fathers Experiencing Newborn Death), 4234 Berrywick Terrace, St. Louis, MO 63128 (314–487–7582).

American Cancer Society, National Office, 90 Park Avenue, New York, NY 10016 (212–599–8200).

American Sudden Infant Death Syndrome Institute, 275 Carpenter Drive, NE, Atlanta, GA 30328 (404–843–1030).

Association for Death Education and Counseling, 638 Prospect Avenue, Hartford, CT 06105 (203–232–4825).

Cancer Information Service, National Cancer Institute, Building 31, Room 10A24, 9000 Rockville Pike, Bethesda, MD 20892 (800–4–CANCER).

Center for Personal Recovery, Dr. Judy Oaks, P.O. Box 125, Berea, KY 40403 (606–986–7878).

Children's Hospice International, Suite 131, 1101 King Street, Alexandria, VA 22314 (800–242–4453).

International Association of Near Death Studies, Box U-20, 406 Cross Campus Road, University of Connecticut, Storrs, CT 06268.

National Hospice Organization, Suite 901, 1900 North Moore Street, Arlington, VA 22209 (703–243–5900).

National Self-Help Resource Center, 2000 South Street, NW, Washington, D.C. 20009.

National Sudden Infant Death Syndrome Clearinghouse, Suite 600, 8201 Greensboro Drive, McLean, VA 22102 (703–821–8955).

Parents of Murdered Children, Inc. (POMC), Unit B-41, 100 East Eighth Street, Cincinnati, OH 45202 (513–721–5683).

Parents of Suicides, Second Floor, 15 East Brinkerhoff Avenue, Palisades Park, NJ 007650 (201–585–7608).

Resolve Through Sharing, Gundersen/Lutheran Medical Center, 1910 South Avenue, LaCrosse, WI 54601 (608–785–0530, ext 3675).

SIDS Alliance, Suite 420, 10500 Little Patuxent Parkway, Columbia, MD 21044 (800–221–SIDS).

Widowed Persons Services, 1909 K Street, NW, Washington, DC 20049 (202–728–4450).

Books (Nonfiction)

Bereavement Support Group Program for Children, B. Haasl and J. Marnocha, Accelerated Development, Inc., 3400 Kilgore Avenue, Muncie, IN 47304 (1–800–222–1166).

The Special Needs of Grieving Children: A Seven-Week Structured Support Group With Resource Section and Bibliography (Units on Grief and Loss For Use With Children and Adolescents In The School Setting), C.D. Harper, R. H. Royer, and G.M. Humphrey, The Grief Support and Education Center, 415 South Main Street, North Canton, OH 44720.

Surviving When Someone You Love Was Murdered: A Professional's Guide to Group Grief Therapy for Families and Friends of Murder Victims, Lula Moshoures Redmond, Psychological Consultation and Education Services, Inc., P. O. Box 6111, Clearwater, FL 34618-6111.

Books (Fiction)

These books can be assigned for book reports or class discussion.

Bridge to Terabithia, Katherine Paterson (death of a close friend).

Christy's Love, Maud Johnson, (teen death due to injury).

Christy's Senior Year, Maud Johnson (death of a boyfriend).

Death Be Not Proud, John Gunther (death of a sibling).

The Egypt Game, Zilpha Snyder (murder of a child and how the neighborhood copes).

The Eyes of the Amaryllis, Natalie Babbitt (grief).

Fall of Freddie the Leaf, Leo Buscaglia.

Hang Tough, Paul Mather, Alfred Slote (terminal illness of a Little League ball player).

Hope for the Flowers, Trina Paulis.

If I Should Die Before I Wake, Lurlene McDaniel (death of a sibling).

I Heard the Owl Call My Name, Margaret Craven (grief).

Love Story, Erich Segal (death of a spouse).

Mask, John Minihan (death, illness, living life to fullest).

A Ring of Endless Light, Madeleine L'Engle (death of a grandparent).

The Secret Garden, Frances H. Burnett (death of a parent, aunt).

There Are Two Kinds of Terrible, Peggy Mann (boy deals with his mother's sudden death).

Tread Softly, Corinne Gerson.

Where the Lilies Bloom, Vera and Bill Cleaver (death of a sibling).

The Yearling, Marjorie K. Rawlings (grief).